OSPREY

Wellington's Peninsula Regiments (1)

The Irish

Mike Chappell

Series editor Martin Windrow

First published in Great Britain in 2003 by Osprey Publishing
Elms Court, Chapel Way, Botley, Oxford OX2 9LP, United Kingdom.
Email: info@ospreypublishing.com

A CIP catalogue record for this book is available from the British Library.

ISBN 1 84176 402 7

Editor: Martin Windrow
Design: Alan Hamp
Index by Alan Rutter
Originated by Electronic Page Company, Cwmbran, UK
Printed in China through World Print Ltd.

03 04 05 06 07   10 9 8 7 6 5 4 3 2 1

FOR A CATALOGUE OF ALL BOOKS PUBLISHED BY
OSPREY MILITARY AND AVIATION PLEASE CONTACT:

The Marketing Manager, Osprey Direct UK
PO Box 140, Wellingborough,
Northants, NN8 2FA, United Kingdom
Email: info@ospreydirect.co.uk

The Marketing Manager, Osprey Direct USA
c/o MBI Publishing, 729 Prospect Avenue
Osceola, WI 54020, USA
Email: info@ospreydirectusa.com

www.ospreypublishing.com

Acknowledgements

The author wishes to thank the Librarian and staff of the Prince Consort's Library, Aldershot, for their help in the preparation of this title. Also Lieutenant-Colonel (retired) Nick Weeks, formerly of the Royal Irish Fusiliers and the Royal Irish Rangers; Captain (retired) W.A. Henshall, Headquarters the Royal Dragoon Guards; and Eric Hunt, author of *Charging Against Napoleon (2001),* Leo Cooper
   All illustrations are from the collection of the author, except where stated otherwise.

Editor's Note

The spelling of the words 'Peninsula/r' often causes confusion. The former is used in this text, as the noun form, in most contexts; conventionally, the adjectival form with a final 'r' is used in the term 'Peninsular War' but rarely elsewhere.

OPPOSITE **Arthur Wellesley, 1st Duke of Wellington (1769–1852), from an engraving of a portrait of 1813. The younger son of an Irish peer, he purchased into the 73rd Highlanders in 1787, and then into several other regiments, becoming a captain in 1791 and a lieutenant-colonel in 1793. He went to India with the 33rd Regiment in 1796, and led a brigade against Tipoo Sahib before becoming governor of Seringapatam and commander of the forces in Mysore. After a series of victories over the Mahrattas he returned to England, was knighted and entered Parliament in 1807. In 1808 he took command of the British expedition to Portugal; after a year 'in the wilderness' after the Convention of Cintra, he was back in Portugal in 1809. From then until 1814 he directed the armies of Britain, Portugal and, to some extent, Spain in a series of campaigns that weakened the French armies in the Peninsula and eventually drove them back over the Pyrenees into France. Wellington was to go on to even greater achievements, but none so glorious as those of the Peninsula.**

WELLINGTON'S PENINSULA REGIMENTS: THE IRISH

THE PENINSULAR WAR

THE HISTORY OF BRITAIN'S standing or regular army is a long and honourable one which reaches back more than three centuries to the restoration of the English monarchy in 1660. In that time its regiments have been sent overseas to fight many wars in the name of their king (or queen), wars from which they have usually returned in triumph, despite often being poorly led, badly prepared and few in number. They continue, quite properly, to take pride in those battles from which they emerged the victors, commemorating their involvement in the likes of Minden, Quebec, Alexandria and Salamanca by marking their anniversaries with parades and feasting. Naturally enough, they rarely celebrate the equally hard-fought contests which they lost (battles such as Fontenoy, 1745, where British troops were forced to retire by a charge delivered by five regiments of the 'Wild Geese' – the Irish Brigade fighting on the side of France).

There are episodes, however, when the achievements of particular British armies so shine from the pages of history that they can only be described as glorious. Perhaps the finest of these was the Peninsular War of 1807–1814 when, led by Sir Arthur Wellesley, later 1st Duke of

Wellington, a small British force fighting beside Portuguese and Spanish allies drove from the Iberian Peninsula the numerically superior forces of Napoleon's France. It was a war of hard fighting over difficult terrain, in which both sides suffered terribly from privation, exhausting marches and an inhospitable climate. As it developed it tied down hundreds of thousands of Napoleon's troops – sorely needed elsewhere, particularly after the disastrous failure of the emperor's Russian campaign of 1812 – in attempts to suppress the insurrection of the people of Spain and to defeat the British-Allied forces. Eventually the French were driven across the Pyrenees and well into the south of their homeland before Napoleon, under pressure elsewhere by the combined forces of Russia, Prussia and Austria, accepted defeat, abdicated and went into exile on Elba in the spring of 1814.

While never aspiring to Napoleon's visionary genius, unleashed by the emperor's absolute political power, in terms of professional soldiering Wellington was arguably the best commander of

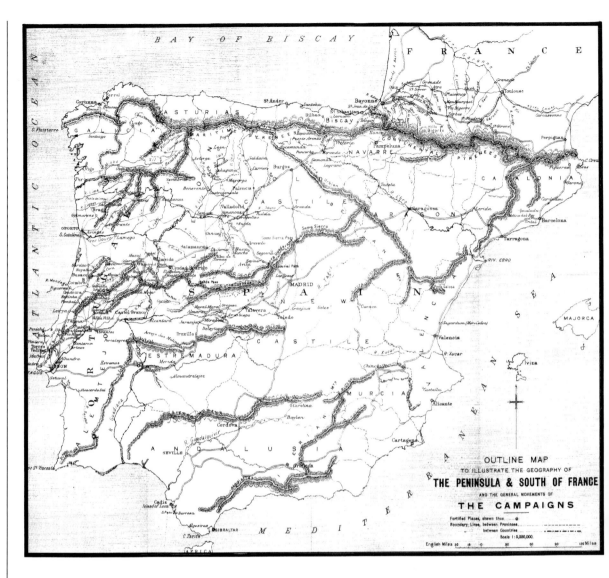

A contemporary map of
Portugal, Spain and southern
France at the time of
the Peninsular War.

his times; and under his leadership the British regiments in the
Peninsula achieved a succession of stunning victories until it seemed
that, with him at their head, they were invincible. Many reasons have
been advanced for this extraordinary flowering of military effectiveness,
but high on any list must be Wellington's talents as a general combined
with British regimental *ésprit de corps* – that special mixture of factors that
produced within a regiment or battalion a level of morale which enabled
it to endure the shock of battle and fight on until the enemy broke. At a
time when soldiers of other armies sought inspiration from political
idealism, the worship of their God and his saints, or the praise of their
emperor, the British soldier looked no further for that which sustained
him than his regiment. His comrades, his leaders, the regimental colours
and title were (and still are) tangible things, more suited to a British
character which even today finds satisfaction and enjoyment in clubs,
pubs and the communal 'support' of sports.

However, they came by their fighting spirit, Wellington's Peninsula
regiments served him well, winning 19 pitched battles and innumerable

other combats, laying ten sieges and taking four great fortresses, and killing, wounding or capturing 200,000 of the enemy to bring the duke his honours, position and great wealth. All they asked in return was for 'that bugger with the long nose' to lead them to further victories (especially if these brought them 'the spoils of war' – prize money, plunder and drink). He rarely failed to do so; but the cost was great. Forty thousand of his men died during his campaigns, their bodies thrown naked (since their clothes had value) into unmarked graves, rivers or pyres, or simply left for the wolves and crows.

The account that follows tells the story of a number of these regiments as they marched and fought in Portugal, Spain and France. Treading the dusty roads behind their fifes and drums, they croaked the songs of the day – 'The Young May Moon', 'Hearts of Oak', and one that may serve as their epitaph:

> *'Over the hills and far away,*
> *To Flanders, Portugal and Spain,*
> *King George commands and we obey,*
> *Over the hills and far away ...'*

THE IRISH REGIMENTS

It has been estimated that 40 per cent of Britain's army at the time of the Napoleonic Wars were Irish, an astounding statistic given the state of turmoil prevailing in Ireland at that time. In order to appreciate just how astounding, a brief description of that unrest is necessary.

In the late 18th century the echoes of the revolution that had seized France were being heard elsewhere in Europe, and particularly in Ireland. 'Liberty, equality and fraternity' were principles desperately sought by that country's poor, who included four million disenfranchised Roman Catholics who could not buy or sell land, bear arms, teach, practice law, join the army or navy, or be involved in politics. Publications such as Tom Paine's *The Rights of Man* and (the Protestant) Wolf Tone's *An argument on behalf of the Catholics in Ireland* fuelled unrest as political societies sprang into being. The 'Society of United Irishmen' campaigned openly for radical reform and the limitation of English influence, and – to a lesser extent – the re-instatement of Irish Catholics into the political nation. Less public were their ultimate aims of independence and republicanism.

'United Irishmen in Training', an English political cartoon of the late 18th century. The reality of what followed the rising of 1798 was far from funny, and extremely bloody.

5

Detail of the centre of the regimental colour of the French 70e Demi-Brigade, taken at Ballinamuck in 1798 when Général Humbert surrendered his landing force.

Underground political groups with widely differing ambitions abounded, most using intimidation to gain their ends. As tension grew the British government in London was warned that the only way to counter the 'French ideas' that had taken hold was to make concessions to the Catholics of Ireland, regardless of the position of the Irish Parliament in Dublin. These began to be made in 1793, and included the disbanding of the old Volunteer movement, and its replacement with a Militia controlled by the government. Catholics were permitted to enlist in this force, a move that effectively put arms into their hands and fanned the flames of sectarian tension. Clashes between Catholic 'Defenders' and Protestant 'Peep-o'-Day Boys' led to the formation of the Loyal Orange Order which, on 12 July 1796, staged its first mass march to commemorate the Protestant King William III's victory at the Battle of the Boyne in 1690. This demonstration was watched with foreboding by the British authorities, who were pre-occupied with the suppression of the clandestine activities of the military wing of the United Irishmen and the Defenders – both of which were actively stoking the fires of rebellion.

The task of maintaining the peace in Ireland was the duty of the British regiments stationed there, acting in aid to the civil power. To this task was soon added that of defence against a threatened invasion by French forces. When Wolf Tone fled from Ireland in 1795 he managed to persuade the French that Ireland was Britain's weak spot, and that landings by French troops would bring about a massive uprising that would drive the British out. In 1796 Tone sailed for Ireland with a French force, eagerly awaited by most in a country that was by then on the brink of civil war; the British Army was at full stretch, the Militia was infiltrated by United Irishmen, and the power of the Orange Order was growing. In the event it was the weather that defeated this first French expeditionary force by preventing its landing, but the threat gave concern to the government and heart to the potential rebels.

An Insurrection Act of 1796 enabled Lord Lieutenants to proclaim areas to be 'in a state of disturbance', thus allowing searches, curfews, press-ganging of the 'idle and disorderly', the calling-out of Yeomanry (militia cavalry), and the billeting of troops in the homes of suspects without repayment. As more and more areas were proclaimed to be in a state of disturbance, pressure grew on the United Irishmen to act before it was too late to do so. In early 1798 they rose, and a bloodbath ensued as the hated Yeomanry – along with innocent Protestants – were slaughtered by Catholic rebels, while Protestant insurrectionists took revenge. The newly raised Militia also behaved badly: 'contemptible before the enemy', they treated cruelly the 'poor wretches' who fell into their hands. Eventually, the main rebel force was defeated at the battle of Vinegar Hill in Wexford in June 1798, two months before the expected French 'invasion' landed in Donegal and County Mayo. In the latter landing the forces of the French General Humbert drove off a force of Militia, Fencibles and regulars at Castlebar, but did not receive the popular support that had been promised. Disheartened, the French clashed with the Limerick Militia at Collooney before being cornered by a superior force and obliged to surrender at Ballinamuck.

The '98 rebellion was over, but not the reprisals. It was estimated that 50,000 people lost their lives in the violence, and to prevent any further outbreak English Militia regiments were brought in to keep the uneasy peace. (One of the military casualties of the rebellion was the 5th Royal Irish Dragoons, who were found to be infiltrated by subversives who had plotted to murder their officers. The regiment was disbanded in 1799.) Wolf Tone, captured along with the French invading force, committed suicide rather than hang. With his death the idealistic philosophy of non-sectarian republicanism faded, and Ireland was absorbed into the Union of Great Britain in 1801.

Fleeing Ireland to escape retribution for their part in the rebellion, a number of Irishmen sought sanctuary in France and employment in the ranks of its army. Taking foreign pay had become a tradition followed by thousands of Irish soldiers of fortune, who over the years had sold their services to countries other than England, where their Catholic religion precluded them from commissions or enlistment. Mostly they went to serve in the armies of France, Austria and Spain; but whilst the Irish Regiments Irlanda, Hibernia and Ultonia were still in Spanish service at the time of the outbreak of the Peninsular War, those regiments of the Irish Brigade serving the French monarchy had lost their foreign identity by being mustered as numbered regiments of the line in 1791. A second abortive uprising took place in Dublin in 1803, followed by a fresh exodus of Irish refugees, which prompted Napoleon to sanction the raising of an Irish battalion, later an 'Irish Legion'.

Against such a background of political turmoil, religious intolerance, repression and war it seems incredible that any Irishman should have sought to serve King George III as a soldier of the British Army; yet very large numbers did so. At a time when army enlistment was entirely voluntary there was a steady flow of Irish Catholic recruits throughout the period of the Napoleonic Wars, and these men filled the gaps in the ranks of English and Scottish regiments, regardless of their new subsidiary titles.

What follows is the story of those units which served in the Peninsula that were raised in Ireland, with ranks mostly filled with Irishmen, and with subsidiary titles (official or unofficial) that proudly proclaimed an Irish identity – two regiments of cavalry and six battalions of infantry. Most served under the direct command of Wellington, while others supported his army in operations in southern and eastern Spain. Their titles, from the Army Lists of the time, were:

The 4th (or Royal Irish) Regiment of Dragoon Guards.

The 18th Regiment of (Light) Dragoons (Hussars) – sometimes called 'King's Irish Hussars'.

The 27th (or Enniskillen) Regiment of Foot – sometimes spelled 'Inniskilling' – with 1st, 2nd and 3rd Battalions.

The 87th (or The Prince of Wales's Irish) Regiment of Foot, from 1811 (The Prince of Wales's Own Irish) – 2nd Battalion.

The 88th (or Connaught Rangers) Regiment of Foot – 1st and 2nd Battalions.

THE 4th ROYAL IRISH DRAGOON GUARDS

Compared with the records of most other Peninsula regiments the 4th Dragoon Guards may be said to have had – to use a World War II expression – a 'bad war'. Dogged by sickness amongst men and horses, handicapped by poor leadership and subject to sheer bad luck, the regiment was unhorsed and sent home under humiliating circumstances after only 21 months' service.

Raised in 1685, the regiment had undergone a number of changes of title before becoming the 1st Irish Horse in 1746 and the 4th Royal Irish Regiment of Dragoon Guards in 1788. By 1811 the regiment was described as 'heavy cavalry' (big men on big horses), with recent service in troubled Ireland and in the north of England, where it had been successful in putting down riots amongst the miners of Northumberland and Durham.

On 26 June 1811 the regiment was stationed at Bristol when it received orders to mobilise six of its ten troops for service under Wellington in the Peninsula. With the 5th Dragoon Guards and the 3rd Dragoons it was to form a brigade of heavy cavalry under the command of Major-General John Le Marchant. In July the six service troops marched to Plymouth for embarkation. They mustered 550 officers and men and 534 horses formed into two squadrons; the remaining four troops were left in England as a depot for those on service. Commanding the 4th Dragoon Guards at the time was Lieutenant-Colonel Francis Sherlock, an officer with 18 years' service who had assumed command in 1809.

After a safe voyage of 11 days the regiment disembarked at Lisbon on 4 August and marched to the base at Belem to form up as a brigade with its fellow regiments. It was here that its misfortunes began as men began to fall ill with 'the Diarheas' (dysentery) brought on, it was believed, by over-indulgence in the abundance of fruit available, and an excessive intake of the local wines. Outbreaks of sickness were not an uncommon occurrence for regiments serving in Portugal and Spain. The primitive sanitation of camp and bivouac life meant that flies spread disease rapidly, while water was used with little consideration as to what disease it might carry. The troopers of the 4th Dragoon Guards were mostly healthy Irish country lads who had had no time to build up the immunity that seemed to keep the sick lists of veteran regiments low; consequently they fell sick almost to a man.

By October 1811 Le Marchant's brigade was at Castello Branco, where it was seen by Wellington; he wrote, 'I yesterday saw the 4th Dragoon Guards. Of 470 men they could produce only 230 mounted, and these looked more like men come of the hospitals, than troops just arrived from England … All the newly arrived regiments of cavalry are in nearly the same state'. Two weeks later he wrote, 'the 4th Dragoon Guards do not get better, and particularly that their continued sickness should be attributed to that extraordinary circumstance in this army "bad food"'. Wellington showed his doubts that diet was the problem; his attitude towards excessive drinking is well known.

The onset of the bitter Peninsula winter added to the burdens of the men of the regiment still at duty. Frequently soaked by rain and sleet, they struggled to manage their own horses and those of the men on the sick list, but the animals were beginning to suffer and lose condition. This was due partly to problems with the supply of fodder, but the real problem was the way the British Army pampered its horses in peacetime – treating them, in many respects, better than its men. Used to comfortable stables, an excellent diet and the best of care, these horses responded badly to the sea journey to Portugal and to campaign conditions in the hostile climate and terrain of the Peninsula. Usually picketed in the open, they rapidly deteriorated – a situation compounded by the sickness that dogged the 4th Dragoon Guards, which left the fit troopers with as many as three horses each to look after. This meant that at times the regiment could field barely more than a single troop of mounted men.

1812

In January 1812 Wellington moved to lay siege to the frontier fortresses of Ciudad Rodrigo and Badajoz, obstacles that barred the way to an advance into Spain. The 4th Dragoon Guards were deployed as part of the screening force to these operations, but shortly after the fall of Ciudad Rodrigo later that month they were transferred from Gen. Le Marchant's brigade. Still able to field only 200 all ranks, the regiment marched to join the brigade of heavy cavalry commanded by Major-General John Slade – and this transfer moved them from the command of a general acknowledged as one of the finest leaders of cavalry in the British Army, to that of one notorious for his dull wits and irresolution. 'God-damn-you Jack' Slade was a bad general; and so was the commander of the cavalry division of which his brigade formed part. General Sir William Erskine was 'sometimes a little mad', but it was trusted that 'he will have no fit during the campaign'. Wellington said of Erskine that 'it is impossible to trust his judgement in any critical case'. The luck of the 4th Royal Irish Dragoon Guards was turning from bad to worse.

A modern depiction of the dress of a dragoon of the 4th Royal Irish Dragoon Guards in 1800. By 1811 it had changed very little, with some variation to the lace of the coat, and the addition of chinscales and a 'skull' or metal lining to the hat. (Royal Dragoon Guards)

Wellington's offensive gathered momentum with the capture of Badajoz on 5 April 1812, after which three cavalry brigades – Slade's, Le Marchant's and Ponsonby's – were sent in pursuit of the French forces withdrawing southwards to Seville. On 11 April, Le Marchant and Ponsonby caught up with 2,000 of the French at Villagarcia near Llerena, and routed them with a series of charges. Slade's brigade was not present at the action, its commander having lost his way; thus the 4th Dragoon Guards lost the opportunity of their first mounted action. When Le Marchant and Ponsonby were ordered to march their brigades north to rejoin the main force under Wellington, Slade's was left with the force containing the French in the south.

On 9 June Wellington sent a dispatch to the commander of this force, which included the following: 'Sir Stapleton Cotton [commanding the cavalry] had ordered the 4th Dragoon Guards to join Le Marchant's brigade, to relieve the 3rd Dragoons, not in very good condition; but I have written to Colonel Sherlock to halt at Niza till you shall send him orders; and you had better order him to join his brigade by easy marches. The regiment is now very strong and in good order.'

The fortunes of Col. Sherlock and the men of the 4th Dragoon Guards were beginning to look up, or so it seemed. Acknowledged to be in good shape by Wellington himself, they had quit the brigade of the dreadful Jack Slade and had marched north to relieve the 3rd Dragoons; but it was at this point that they marched from the pages of recorded history and into the grey mists of speculation, where bad luck still continues to dog them. Official sources deny that they ever joined Le Marchant's brigade, in which the 3rd Dragoons continued to be shown as present. It would seem that Wellington's reference in his letter of 9 June to having written to Sherlock referred to an order given and acted upon before that date; for on 11 June, Gen. Slade fought an action with French cavalry at Maguilla in which only the 3rd Dragoon Guards and the 1st Royal Dragoons took part. (Slade's rare outburst of impetuosity cost him 48 men killed and wounded and 118 taken prisoner. It was Maguilla that caused Wellington to comment on 'the trick our officers of cavalry have acquired of galloping at everything, then galloping back as fast …'.)

By the time of the battle of Salamanca on 22 July six weeks or more had elapsed since the 4th Dragoons rode to relieve the 'not in very good condition' 3rd Dragoons. On the day of the battle Major-General John Gaspard Le Marchant led his brigade in a decisive charge that smashed several French regiments before meeting his death at his moment of triumph. According to the account of a relation of his, having personally cut down six of the enemy Le Marchant placed himself at the head of a 'half-squadron of the 4th Royal Irish Dragoon Guards', and was in the act of driving French stragglers into the forest when he was killed instantly by a shot which cut through his sash and broke his spine. If this account is true, it seems that some of the 4th Dragoon Guards got to Le Marchant's brigade in time for the battle of Salamanca, if only to reinforce the ailing 3rd Dragoons, who were posted as present.

The next recorded sighting of the 4th Dragoon Guards was in Madrid, where they were reported to be for several days at the time when Wellington's forces were besieging Burgos; but for months after the victory at Salamanca none of the standard histories of the Peninsular War make reference to the regiment until the end of the year. What may safely be assumed is that the 4th Dragoon Guards suffered the full rigours of the retreat of Wellington's army after he gave up the siege of Burgos. By the time it reached Portugal and safety in November 1812 that army had lost 9,000 men and had some 16,000 sick. Their horses had suffered appallingly, with large numbers dying from starvation and exhaustion while others, unable to get on, were shot. When safety was reached the surviving horses could scarcely bear the weight of a rider.

Like most cavalry units in Wellington's army in early 1813, the 4th Dragoon Guards were in a bad state. They could parade 311 men for duty, but only 89 fit horses – a sorry pass for the proud regiment that had marched out of Lisbon barely 18 months previously. It was the state of their animals that was to seal their fate; they became one of the three regiments nominated to hand over their horses and return home.

Caricature by R.Dighton of Maj.Gen. 'God-damn you Jack' Slade, brigade commander of the unfortunate 4th Royal Irish Dragoon Guards for most of their time in the Peninsula. Slade is depicted in the uniform of the 1st Royal Dragoons; that of the officers of the 4th Dragoon Guards was similar.

By a supreme irony the regiment was informed of its fate on St Patrick's Day 1813, an announcement that must have put a damper on the traditional festivities enjoyed by Irish regiments on that day. Their animals were passed to the other two regiments in their brigade and, in company with the men of the other dismounted regiments, they footslogged the 130 miles to Lisbon before embarkation on 15 April 1813. Their service in the Peninsula had cost the 4th Royal Irish Dragoon Guards the lives of two officers, 239 other ranks and 445 horses – all of whom died of sickness and the rigours of campaigning. It had also earned the regiment its only battle honour, PENINSULA.

It seems extraordinary that despite the millions of words written on the British Army in the Peninsular War, one of its regiments could 'disappear' for several months in the manner of the 4th Dragoon Guards, leaving its whereabouts and doings a matter of speculation and guesswork. The officers and men of the regiment can surely be forgiven for wishing to forget such a sad chapter in their lives, but not the historians.

THE 18th HUSSARS

One of five regiments of light cavalry formed in 1759, this regiment was raised in Ireland and numbered the 19th Light Dragoons. From its formation until its disbandment 62 years later it was popularly known as 'the Drogheda Light Horse' after its colonel, Charles Moore, Earl of Drogheda. It was later renumbered the 18th. Permission was given for the regiment to be clothed and equipped as hussars in December 1807, and in the following July the newly styled 18th Hussars embarked 745 officers and men at Northfleet bound for Portugal and Wellington's army. However, by the time they had landed and were ready for service Wellington was no longer in command, having been superceded and then recalled to England following the infamous Convention of Cintra. The army's new commander was Sir John Moore; and in October 1808, under orders to co-operate with the Spanish armies, he marched his army into Spain.

The disaster that befell Moore and the misery, privation and breakdown of discipline on the retreat to Corunna are perhaps too well known to bear repetition here. For the cavalry, and particularly the 18th Hussars, the campaign brought sharp skirmishing as they screened the rearguard from the pursuing French cavalry, only to have to shoot their horses on the beach at Corunna shortly before embarking for England in January 1809. Divided as they were between a number of vessels, it was some time before the regiment could be re-assembled at Deal, Kent, to compare their scarecrow appearance as horseless survivors with that of the regiment which had left England at full strength, well-mounted and perfectly equipped six months previously.

1813
Five years were to pass before the 'Drogheda Light Horse' would be en route for Portugal again. New Year's Day 1813 found the regiment marching to Portsmouth for embarkation; they sailed on 19 January, suffering an uncomfortable voyage before making landfall at Belem on

3 February. The 18th Hussars were by now commanded by Lt.Col. Henry Murray, and formed a brigade of light cavalry with the 10th and 15th Hussars stationed at Luz and Benfica. Their time was taken up with reviews and preparations for Wellington's forthcoming offensive, whose timing depended to a certain extent on the availability of green fodder in the spring. On 17 March the following order was posted:

'Saint Patrick Day. The Retrait will not sound tonight till 10 o'clock at which every Man must return quietly home. Ireland looks to the 18th as Pecularly her own, to uphold her name by their good conduct abroad, and she has had reasons to be proud that they did belong to her. But on the long list of Crimes, discreditable and mean, which of late have prevailed in the Regiment, their Country can look with no feelings, but those of Humiliation & Regret. It is hoped however that the recurance of the Festival of their Patron Saint will recall to the recollection of every Irish Soldier that a high sense of honour above every mean or dishonest action is equally characteristic, with undaunted courage & nature of a True born Irishman.'

Despite these noble words an officer of the regiment noted in his diary, 'Many broken heads in the Regiment this evening: one man carried in the hospital more dead than alive'. That time hung heavy for all the regiments in the locality is reflected in the record of acts of indiscipline amongst the officers, non-commissioned officers and men, mostly due to the cheapness of drink in the Lisbon area. On 18 May the 18th Hussars' brigade was reviewed by Wellington, who expressed himself 'highly pleased' at their appearance (he was to have cause to change his opinion the following month).

On 31 May 1813, after a hazardous crossing of the River Esla, the regiment surprised a piquet of French dragoons and captured 50 including their commander. Eventually the 18th Hussars, with the other regiments of their brigade, caught up with the enemy rearguard at Morales where, on 2 June, an action was fought against three regiments of French dragoons. Both

Charles Hamilton-Smith print of a dragoon of the 18th Hussars at about the time of the departure of the regiment for their second tour in the Peninsula. The dress and equipment are essentially that described in the commentary to Plate A as for 'review order'.

sides became mixed together in a killing match in which it was 'impossible to distinguish the enemy from our own hussars … The whole plain in ten minutes presented a dreadful scene: dead, wounded and prisoners in all directions – I never saw men so mad for action as the hussars were …'. The enemy retired having lost 220 men taken prisoner and as many horses, leaving their dead and wounded on the field. Wellington called the action a 'very handsome affair'.

The French continued their withdrawal to the north, with the British cavalry hard on their heels; the pursuers' progress was marred by outbreaks of indiscipline which plagued the army – especially looting, for which two men of the 18th Hussars received 600 lashes each. (By now Lt.Col. Murray had retired sick, and command of the regiment was assumed by Maj. James Hughes.) Closing up on the fortress of Burgos, the regiment were involved in a skirmish with the enemy at Isar on 12 June before pushing on towards Vittoria, where the French army stood to do battle.

As dawn broke on 21 June 1813 the 18th Hussars took post with their brigade. Looking over the broad valley of the River Zadorra they could see through the mist and rain the entire French position; this extended several miles either side of a commanding hill on which Joseph, brother of the Emperor Napoleon and King of Spain, could be seen with his staff. Fighting began on the enemy's left at about 8.30am, when their troops holding high ground were attacked and driven from their positions. Two hours later the sounds of battle from the French right rear gave evidence that the force under Gen. Graham was pursuing Wellington's orders to block the French line of retirement. At about midday Wellington ordered his centre to cross the Zadorra and start driving the French back on the town of Vittoria. Bitter fighting ensued, and continued until about 5pm when the beaten French began to retire from the battlefield. The retirement became a rout, and as every man attempted to save himself the entire baggage train of King Joseph's army and court was abandoned.

The plunder accumulated by the puppet monarch of Spain during the years of his reign lay before the advancing British, begging to be taken; and taken it was. Gold, silver and jewels disappeared into the pockets, knapsacks, haversacks and valises of the retiring French and the advancing British, Portuguese and Spanish in a frenzy of looting. Nothing could stop it, and the battle came to a halt, allowing large numbers of the defeated French to escape. Wellington was furious at the behaviour of his men and sought to make example of those who had misbehaved. During the closing moments of the battle he encountered men of the 18th Hussars drunk and looting in the streets of Vittoria, and this incident was to focus his attention on the regiment more than any other.

The 18th Hussars had begun the battle as part of the central thrust across the Zadorra, harassing the retiring French while a fierce artillery duel raged. Several charges against infantry were carried out, including one against a square, with shot, shell and musketry causing the Hussars many casualties before the squadrons were recalled to let the infantry press on. As the enemy broke the 18th Hussars were again called forward to take up the pursuit. Galloping over the field of battle they passed the dead and wounded of the infantry combat and the guns, limbers and ammunition wagons abandoned by the fleeing French gunners, before arriving at the town of Vittoria. Entering the town, they clattered through the streets amidst the chaos of an exultant Spanish population and the resistance of the remnants of the retreating French. On reaching the outward gate of the town leading to the Pamplona road they came upon 'the whole of the Royal and French general's equipage consisting of many coaches. Treasure chests, wagons, carts, numberless servants in the Royal livery, the finest horses and mules, seemed here assembled: even King Joseph himself … had been in this same spot but a few minutes before … the Spaniards were taking advantage of the general confusion and immediately set to breaking open the treasure chests – literally strewing the ground with bags of doubloons and dollars – jewels, watches, trinkets and all sorts of plunder …'

After a skirmish with a body of Joseph's Guards the 18th Hussars took up the pursuit until nightfall, when the roll call showed that they had lost 11 killed and 23 wounded that day. The pursuit continued; but on 24 June the regiment was paraded and the men searched for plunder, of which a great deal was found and given to the paymaster for the 'general benefit of the Regiment'. It was at about this time that the first indications were received that Wellington had seen men of the regiment misbehaving in the streets of Vittoria. He was later to write, '… our vagabond soldiers … have got among them about a million sterling in money… instead of … getting rest and food to prepare them for the pursuit they spend the night looking for plunder … The 18th Hussars are a disgrace to the name of soldier, in action as well as elsewhere …' The duke threatened that any further misconduct would result in the regiment being dismounted and sent home.

It was sheer bad luck that Wellington had happened upon a few 18th Hussars as he did; other regiments had looted as brazenly, and most of 'Drogheda's Cossacks' – as they were fond of referring to themselves – had done their duty under difficult circumstances, continuing the pursuit as ordered. But they stood condemned by the behaviour of their opportunist comrades, both those observed by Wellington and the 20 men under a Lt. Dolbell who, having been ordered to guard the captured baggage train, immediately set about plundering it. (Mr Dolbell had the misfortune of being reported to Wellington by a French general's wife who claimed that he had robbed her of her rings.) Perhaps the most famous piece of loot taken by the 18th Hussars was the baton of Marshal Jourdan, found by Cpl. Fox, who unscrewed the gold caps but allowed the shaft to fall into the hands of a drummer of the 2/87th. Its parts re-united, the baton was eventually presented to the Prince Regent, along with other trophies taken at the battle.

Late July 1813 found the 18th Hussars marching north to Pamplona, where the French garrison was under siege. Enemy relief columns attempting to raise the siege had reached Sorauren a few miles away, and before these the 18th took post, skirmishing with the French cavalry on the Allied right. On the 30th, Wellington's counter-attack drove the French relieving force back across the Pyrenees in what was principally an infantry battle, while the 18th Hussars continued to provide a flank guard.

By early October Wellington's forces had crossed the River Bidassoa and had entered France. In early November, after the wretched garrison of Pamplona had capitulated, the 18th Hussars also marched to the valley of the Bidassoa and the frontier of France. Winter was setting in as men and horses picked their way over precipitous tracks through the mountains; it was at this time that the regiment dropped even lower in Wellington's esteem when he caught an 18th Hussar in the act of stealing a sheep.

December 1813 found the 18th on French soil, patrolling the River Nive beyond which the enemy had retired. Skirmishing with French outposts and patrols enlivened a duty made miserable by the weather, until on the 9th of the month Wellington's troops began to force a

Hamilton-Smith print of men, horses and a vehicle of the 'Waggon Train' at the time of the Peninsular War. In 1808, Wellington took with him as part of his expedition to Portugal two troops of the Irish Waggon Train, but their separate identity does not seem to have survived long.

passage of the river. This action involved the 18th Hussars in harrying enemy retirements, rounding up prisoners, and clashing with any French cavalry interfering with the operations of the Allied infantry and guns. On 18 December two squadrons of the 18th Hussars supported Spanish troops in an 'excursion' against the French at Mendionde. On 22 December the regiment marched to winter quarters at Hasparren, where they remained until February 1814.

1814

With Wellington's resumption of offensive operations the French were driven back from river line to river line until, having lost contact with their garrison at Bayonne, they turned to do battle at Orthez. On the heels of the enemy as they retired were the Allied cavalry including the 18th Hussars, whose route between 14 February and the end of that month took them across four rivers in pursuit of the French.

On 26 February the 18th Hussars caught up with the enemy rearguard (the 15e Chasseurs à Cheval) near Puyoo and instantly charged, pursuing the enemy for 'half a league' whilst cutting at them and taking many prisoners and horses. On the 27th the French were found to be drawn up for battle before the town of Orthez. Fighting began at about 8.30am and went on until about 2pm, by which time the enemy had been defeated and began retiring on Toulouse. It had been an affair of infantry and guns for Wellington's force, his cavalry not becoming involved until the closing stages of the battle. For the 18th Hussars the day began with the flogging of seven men, after which they remained spectators to events while sheltering from the artillery fire that came their way. With the retreat of the French the 18th Hussars followed in pursuit but not in close contact. An officer observed, 'The road was strewn with corpses, more, I believe, than at Vittoria; and for the time the battle lasted, it was one of the biggest slaughters of the campaign.' (Wellington is said to have suffered 2,164 casualties to the French 4,000 – which included 1,350 prisoners. The highest casualties suffered by a

British regiment in this battle were the 269 of the 1/88th Connaught Rangers, caught in line by a squadron of French Chasseurs.)

The pursuit of the enemy continued, while a force that included the 18th Hussars marched on Bordeaux to secure that city's surrender. The regiment did not get to enter Bordeaux, which capitulated on 12 March; instead they guarded crossings of the River Garonne. On the 15th orders were received for the regiment to march with reinforcements to counter a French excursion from Toulouse. St Patrick's Day was spent in the saddle, sober, and by the 20th the noises of a battle could be heard from the direction of Tarbes. 'Drogheda's Cossacks' steeled themselves to join it, but the French slipped away and retired on Toulouse once again. (It was at this time that the 18th Hussars were joined by an extra squadron from England.)

Wellington now marshalled his forces to strike at Toulouse. As the army moved up on that city the cavalry provided a screen about the marching columns of men and guns. On 28 March the 18th Hussars clashed with enemy outposts at St Martin du Touche, under the walls of Toulouse, and on charging came under fire from the guns of the city; the leading squadron was lucky to escape with the loss of only one man and four horses.

On 8 April the regiment captured a bridge at Croix d'Orade by means of a bold charge which took the defending French cavalry by surprise, broke them and drove them off the bridge with the loss of 120 prisoners. The whole incident was witnessed by Wellington, and went a long way towards restoring the reputation of the 18th Hussars.

On 10 April, the day of the battle of Toulouse, the regiment were ordered to move along the banks of the River Ers to try to seize one of its bridges. In doing so they encountered the French 22e Chasseurs and Schonbrun Hussars, whom they charged and put to flight; but once again, the issue was decided by a combat of infantry and guns, and by 4.30pm the French began abandoning their positions and falling back. On the following morning they made preparations to evacuate Toulouse, a feat carried out on the night of 11 April. The irony of Wellington's victory was not only that it cost him 4,558 casualties compared to the 3,236 of the French, but that it need not have been fought at all – unknown to both Wellington and Marshal Soult, Napoleon had abdicated on 6 April.

For the officers and men of 'Drogheda's Cossacks' there remained the long march through France with the rest of Wellington's cavalry before crossing the Channel for home. Their exploits in Spain and France were subsequently considered worthy of only the single battle honour PENINSULA in April 1815; to what extent this was due to Wellington's low opinion of the regiment is still open to speculation.

Wellington's achievement in the Peninsular War would not have been possible without the support and co-operation of the Portuguese and Spanish peoples. In this drawing of 1809 a private of the Royal Police Guard of Lisbon (note the interesting holster for a pair of pistols) and a member of the Algarve Ordenanza are depicted at musketry practice. (See MAA 346, *The Portuguese Army of the Napoleonic Wars (2)*, p.36, and MAA 358, *The Portuguese Army ... (3)*, p.10.

THE 27th (ENNISKILLEN) REGIMENT OF FOOT

The 27th was the second most senior of all the infantry regiments claiming to be Irish. It traced its history back to 1689, when Maj. Zacharia Tiffin received a commission to raise a regiment of foot for the service of King William of Orange and the defence of the town of Enniskillen or Inniskilling. In 1751 it was numbered as the 27th (Enniskillen) Regiment, and in 1800 a second battalion was formed. Briefly disbanded, the 2/27th was re-raised in 1804, and a third battalion was formed in 1805. All three battalions were to serve in the Peninsula, the 1/27th and 2/27th in south-eastern Spain and the 3/27th under Wellington. At the end of the war the 1st, 2nd and 3rd Bns were united in southern France before being dispersed to England and Canada.

The 1/27th and 2/27th

Both battalions were serving in the Mediterranean area at the time Wellesley and his army landed in Portugal. As the war against the French developed it was decided in 1812 to form an Allied army in south-eastern Spain for operations against the French. Both the 1/27th and 2/27th were selected to join this force, sailing from Sicily and landing at Alicante in late 1812 and early 1813.

The 1/27th joined one of the divisions of the Allied force (which included British, German, Swiss, Italian and Sicilian troops, as well as the Spanish armies with which they were to co-operate); but the 2nd Bn were chosen to act as light infantry, part of a 'light brigade' consisting of the 2/27th, the light and rifle companies of the 3rd and 8th Bns of the King's German Legion, the Calabrese Free Corps, a brigade of pack artillery, and a squadron of 'Foreign Hussars' – mostly French, Hungarian and Polish deserters.

Once assembled, the Allied force marched north seeking contact with the French. In the lead was the light brigade, and at Alcoy on 6 March 1813 they clashed with the enemy incurring 17 casualties, one of whom was Capt. Parsons of the light company (see Plate E2). Nine days later the grenadier company of the 2/27th under Capt. Waldron (see Plate E1) drove a superior force of the enemy from the village of Alsafara, but these actions were merely skirmishes before the main event.

On 11 April 1813 news was received that the main French force was advancing. The commander of the Allied light brigade disposed his force in and around the village of Biar and met the advancing enemy, inflicting casualties on them before withdrawing through the pass of Biar, battling all the while with their light troops and a body of cuirassiers. The latter were ambushed in the confines of the pass; it was noted that British musket balls shot into the cuirassiers at point-blank range passed through breastplates, bodies and backplates before exiting. This slaughter was performed by three companies of the 2/27th. After this last encounter the French left the light brigade unmolested as they marched back to the Allied main position at Castalla. It had been 'a very pretty fight' in which the 2/27th had acquitted themselves well.

Battle of Castalla, from sketch at Horse Guards.

A contemporary drawing of the action by the 2/27th Regiment on the Heights of Guerra on 13 April 1813, captioned 'Battle of Castalla from sketch at Horse Guards'. The original key is as follows: 'A, Castalla; B, Unit, French Cavalry; C, Spaniards coming back; D, French Column; E, 27th; F, Colonel Adam; G, Part of the 8th Company of the 27th detached to fill up a gap left by the Spaniards; H, Village of Tibi'.

On 13 April the French deployed three divisions before the Allied line at Castalla, which was centred on the castle of Castalla and a ridge called the Heights of Guerra. It was upon this ridge that both the 1/27th and 2/27th took post. The battle began with a French attack on the Spanish troops holding the extremity of the heights, with the intention of rolling up the Allied line along the ridge from that flank. But the Spaniards halted the enemy, as did the 2/27th fighting beside them. Coming under fire from the 2/27th, the colonel of the French 121e Régiment de Ligne gave orders for his leading companies to deploy from column into line, and while this manoeuvre was being performed an extraordinary event took place.

A grenadier officer of the 121e stepped forward and challenged 'any English officer' to single combat. Captain Waldron of the 2/27th, 'an agile Irishman of boiling courage', took him up on his challenge and the pair went at it, as their swords 'clashed and glittered' in the sunshine. A cut that cleft the Frenchman's head ended the duel; Waldron just had time to pick up his adversary's sword before his battalion raced downhill in a bayonet charge that drove the enemy before them as a disorganised mob. As a consequence of this rout the French columns attempting to outflank the Allied position also fell back and the French commander ordered his force to retire over the pass of Biar. The battle of Castalla proved to the French forces in south-eastern Spain that they had a formidable force confronting them. Far from being able to send troops to the aid of those confronting Wellington, they had to draw in reinforcements to bolster up the force confronting the Allies.

In June 1813 an Allied force was landed at Tarragona to lay siege to that fortress, but it retired when a French relieving force approached. In

September an action was fought in the pass of Ordell in which the 2/27th – the only British unit present – suffered over 300 casualties in a desperate fight to hold the position before falling back on the main body at Villa Franca. This place was also given up after a battle in which the 1/27th took part. In February 1814 a blockade of Barcelona was commenced, in which both battalions took part. This was given up in April, and the two units were ordered to march to join the army of the Duke of Wellington in southern France.

The 3/27th

This battalion was embodied in Edinburgh on 25 September 1805 from the supernumeraries thrown up by successful recruiting for the 2/27th. The 3rd Bn was composed chiefly of young men and lads, giving rise to the nickname of the 'Young Enniskillens'. It began life in Scotland as a 'holding and drafting' battalion for the two senior battalions of the regiment, moving to Belfast in December 1806, then to Omagh and, in July 1807, to Enniskillen. In September 1808 the 3/27th embarked for Portugal, 800 strong and under the command of Lt.Col. Maclean. They landed at Lisbon on 2 November, having contracted 'severe fever' during their long time on board the ships, and they were to take some time to recover. By January 1810 they were fit enough to join a brigade of the 4th Division at Guarda, where they remained until the Anglo-Portuguese army under Wellesley fell back upon the Busaco position in September. In the battle that took place there on the evening of 26 September and the day of the 27th, the battalion, posted on the extreme left of the Anglo-Portuguese line, were not engaged and

A vivid drawing by Cecil C.P.Lawson of the incident during the battle of Castalla when Captain Waldron of the 2/27th engaged in single combat with a French officer. Although not a contemporary drawing it follows the 'sketch at Horse Guards' faithfully.

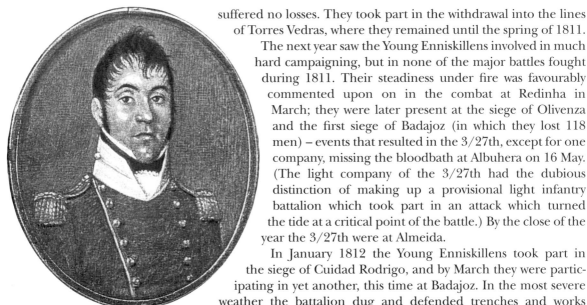

John Waldron, the 'Irishman of boiling courage'. Miniature portraits such as this were often painted before an officer left for service in the Peninsula; in this case Waldron is depicted wearing a field officer's pair of epaulettes rather than a flank company captain's pair of wings, so the portrait post-dates his exploit at Castalla.

suffered no losses. They took part in the withdrawal into the lines of Torres Vedras, where they remained until the spring of 1811.

The next year saw the Young Enniskillens involved in much hard campaigning, but in none of the major battles fought during 1811. Their steadiness under fire was favourably commented upon on in the combat at Redinha in March; they were later present at the siege of Olivenza and the first siege of Badajoz (in which they lost 118 men) – events that resulted in the 3/27th, except for one company, missing the bloodbath at Albuhera on 16 May. (The light company of the 3/27th had the dubious distinction of making up a provisional light infantry battalion which took part in an attack which turned the tide at a critical point of the battle.) By the close of the year the 3/27th were at Almeida.

In January 1812 the Young Enniskillens took part in the siege of Cuidad Rodrigo, and by March they were participating in yet another, this time at Badajoz. In the most severe weather the battalion dug and defended trenches and works that were part of the artillery operations to batter breaches in the walls prior to an infantry assault. On 6 April these breaches were considered to be practicable, and Wellington ordered Badajoz to be stormed. Such was the enemy firepower and the stubborness of the garrison's resistance to the stormers of the 4th Division that their attack failed. However, the French concentration of their forces at the breaches allowed the besiegers to escalade the walls elsewhere and, after a night of savage fighting, the enemy surrendered as dawn broke. In their valiant but futile attempt to storm Badajoz the 3/27th sustained 298 casualties.

By late June the battalion was marching deeper into Spain, and on 18 July they made a gallant charge against a strong French column and 'put it to flight'. On 22 July, at the battle of Salamanca, Wellington placed the 3/27th atop the 'English' Arapile – one of the two hills dominating the field – and ordered Col. Maclean, 'You must defend this position as long as you have a man'. The battalion did so, throughout the turmoil of the battle, until Wellington obtained his great victory and the French army was in full retreat. The 3/27th followed the enemy and entered Madrid with Wellington's army to share in a tumultuous welcome; but within weeks they were marching back to the Portuguese frontier through wind and rain, short of rations, and in some cases barefoot, after Wellington was forced to give up his siege of Burgos. Thousands of men were lost to fatigue and exposure and discipline began to break down, but the Young Enniskillens lost only four men during the retreat – a testimony to the fortitude and discipline of the battalion. At Villa de Corvo the 3/27th went into winter quarters.

From the summer of 1813 until the spring of the following year the 3/27th were to spend ten months marching and fighting in a series of battles that were to eject Napoleon's armies from Spain and carry the war into the French homeland. At Vittoria on 21 June 1813 the Young Enniskillens found themselves pursuing a beaten enemy; this they did with a will, sustaining only 44 casualties. (History does not record if any of the officers or men of the 3/27th laid hands on the plunder which abounded after the battle.) Following up the French, the battalion took part in the blockade of the fortress of Pamplona until the middle of July, when it again marched in pursuit of the retreating French. At Roncesvalles the enemy turned to do battle on 24 July, forcing the Allies to fall back on Pamplona. In the 4th Division the 3/27th acted as rearguard. In late July the French severely pressed the position held by the 4th Division, and were equally severely repulsed. Referring to what was to be called the battle of the Pyrenees, Wellington wrote, 'The battle now became general along the whole front of … the 4th Division, and in every part in our favour, excepting where one battalion of the 10th Portuguese were posted. This battalion having been overpowered … the enemy established themselves on our line … I, however, ordered the 27th and 48th Regiment to charge … Both attacks succeeded, and the enemy was driven down with immense loss.'

At the storming of St Sebastian on 31 August 1813 a detachment of the 3/27th volunteered for the 'forlorn hope'. Lieutenant Harding, its leader, was killed with many of his men while behaving 'gallantly' in the breach.

On 10 November the Young Enniskillens formed part of the attack on the enemy positions on the River Nivelle. In a day's fierce fighting the French were driven out, losing 51 pieces of cannon, many dead and wounded and 1,400 prisoners. In December, Wellington's men crossed another defended river line on the Nive before going into winter quarters, this time on French territory.

In late February 1814 the 3/27th were back in action at Orthez, where they helped take the village of St Boes before participating in the assault on the French main position and the pursuit after its defeat.

The last battle of the 3/27th was that of Toulouse. At 8am on 10 April 1814 the battalion had the honour of leading its column into the attack, of remaining steady under the fire of artillery and musketry for the whole day, of being threatened by cavalry to its flank, of forming the left of the Allied line, and of losing 106 officers and men killed or wounded. When the French evacuated Toulouse the 3/27th were preparing to follow them when news was received of the abdication of Napoleon – the Peninsular War was at an end. The Young Enniskillens marched instead for Bordeaux, where they were to be united with the 1st and 2nd Bns of their regiment. Between them the three units shared the following battle honours for the Peninsular War, most of them earned by the 3rd Battalion: PENINSULA, BADAJOZ, SALAMANCA, VITTORIA, PYRENEES, NIVELLE, ORTHES, TOULOUSE.

THE 87th (THE PRINCE OF WALES'S OWN IRISH) REGIMENT OF FOOT

The 87th was one of a number of 'war-raised' infantry regiments which came into existence following the outbreak of war with revolutionary France. Several were raised in Ireland, most adopting a subsidiary title reflecting their origins. Major John Doyle, who held the post of secretary to the Prince of Wales, was chosen to raise the 87th in 1793, and obtained the prince's permission to call the regiment 'The Prince of Wales's Irish'. Doyle became Lieutenant-Colonel Commandant of the 87th, leading it during its first campaign.

The 87th had mixed fortunes in its early years, going into captivity in Holland in 1795 and being re-raised before service in the West Indies, South America, South Africa and India. In 1804 a second battalion was raised by Doyle's son in accordance with an Additional Forces Act, and allotted recruiting areas in Tipperary, Galway and Clare. For several years the 2/87th moved between Ireland and England (including a spell in Guernsey, where the now Sir John Doyle was Governor) until, in December 1808, they received orders to embark for the Peninsula, with 35 officers and 1,100 men under the command of Maj. Hugh Gough. As was common in those days the voyage was much delayed by bad weather; consequently it was not until 13 March 1809 that the 2/87th landed at Lisbon.

1809

In May the battalion had an inauspicious introduction to war when, as part of a force led by their fellow Irishman Gen. Beresford, they were led on a madcap forced march over mountain tracks in pouring rain. They failed in their purpose – to catch and bring to battle a retiring French force – but managed to lose food, arms, ammunition and especially shoes in the swollen streams and the mud. Thousands of men fell out of the marching column through sickness, hunger and exhaustion, including 250 men of the 2/87th, and their subsequent behaviour when reported to Sir Arthur Wellesley caused him to brand them, 'a rabble who cannot bear success any more than Sir John Moore's army could bear failure'. He was particularly angry at the behaviour of the 2/87th (and the other Irish regiment in their brigade, the 1/88th Connaught Rangers), and threatened to report them as unfit for service in the field and to send them on garrison duties. However, short as he was of troops, he kept the two Irish battalions, brigading them with five companies of the 5/60th (Royal American) Regiment in Donkin's brigade of the newly-organised 3rd Division.

On 27 June 1809 the 2/87th marched with Wellesley's army on a route that took them up the valley of the River Tagus and into Spain, where they joined up with a Spanish army. The aim of the Allied force was to bring to battle a French army under Marshal Victor. At Talavera on 27 July the 2/87th were part of a screen forward of the Anglo-Spanish main position; it was a hot afternoon, and Col. Donkin had allowed his men to rest in the shade of a wood. Suddenly, volleys of musketry shattered the peaceful scene as a French infantry column surprised them. Wellesley rode into the ensuing chaos to restore the situation, but their lack of vigilance had cost the 2/87th some 200 casualties. By late afternoon Donkin's shaken brigade was back on the main Anglo/Spanish position. (With the Spanish 4th Division at Talavera were two battalions of the Irlanda Regiment; many of this regiment's officers were Irish or of Irish descent, but the number of Irish rank-and-file by this date is unknown.)

At 9pm the French began an attack on that part of the Allied line held by Donkin's men. Eventually three French battalions broke into the British position, but by then it was dark, the fighting was confused, and no authority has ever positively identified the regiment that beat the enemy back (though at least two claim that it was the 2/87th). A nervous night was spent under arms awaiting the next onslaught, which was launched at 5am on the 28th, preceded by heavy and accurate artillery fire. As the French columns once more tramped up the hillsides they were driven back by rolling volleys of British musketry. Between 1 and 2pm the French renewed their attack but, unable to defeat the Allied line, they broke off the battle and marched from a field by then ablaze over a vast area from the shells of the artillery; they had lost 7,000 men to Wellesley's 5,000. The British public claimed Talavera as a victory for their army, and its leader was created Viscount Wellington; but their first battle had cost the 2/87th dear – 354 casualties including their commanding officer, Maj. Hugh Gough, wounded.

With his communications threatened the newly-made viscount marched his men back to the borders of Portugal where, on 24 September, he issued an order criticising the discipline of regiments in his command, and adding that he wished attention paid, 'to the state of discipline (meaning by that word habits of obedience to orders, subordination, regularity, and interior economy) of … the 2nd battalion 87th Regiment, as well as to their parade discipline and drill.'

Lieutenant-Colonel John Doyle at the time of the raising of the 87th (Prince of Wales's Irish) Regiment. The devices on his epaulettes are the Prince of Wales' plumes and motto above the harp of Ireland, reflecting the new regiment's title.

1811

Early in the new year of 1810 the Spanish appealed to the British for help at Cadiz, which was under threat by the French. The 2/87th, by then back up to strength, were sent as part of a force drawn from England, Portugal and Gibraltar. Life as part of the Cadiz garrison consisted mainly of watching the British ships in the harbour bombarding the French batteries on land and vice versa, but early in 1811 an expedition was formed with the aim of striking at the French besiegers from the sea by landing forces in their rear. The 2/87th, under the now recovered Maj. Gough, were selected to be part of the expedition, and embarkation began on 19 February. By the 26th of that month the British contingent, numbering 5,000 men under Gen. Graham, had landed at Tarifa to join a Spanish contingent of 7,000 headed by Gen. La Peña, who then took overall command. La Peña led his force on a long and tiring series of marches and countermarches, mostly by night and through waterlogged terrain, that brought the expedition gradually nearer Cadiz until on 4 March its vanguard encountered the French. He ordered yet another night march, during which his troops stumbled about until the dawn allowed them to find the route they had been seeking – the coastal road beside a feature called Barrosa Hill. It was here that the French struck, falling upon the landward flank and rear of the British columns. General Graham immediately ordered his men to counter-attack, and Maj. Gough and his men of the 2/87th moved back through the wood they were in and deployed into line on its edge under intense fire. Four officers and more than 50 men fell before the battalion was even ready to advance.

(continued on page 33)

The FRENCH IMPERIAL EAGLE,
Taken by SERGEANT MASTERMAN of the 87th Regt in the
Action at BARROSA, March 5th 1811.
Drawn, Etch'd, & Pub. by Dighton, Spring Gardens, May 1811.

Only two months after the battle of Barrosa, Dighton published in London a print representing Sergeant Masterson capturing the Eagle of the French 8e de Ligne. At that remove he could have had no idea of the appearance of the man he portrayed (whom he called 'Masterman') or the details of his uniform; the print therefore cannot be taken either as a likeness, or – probably – as an informed representation of his dress. Interestingly, however, the Eagle is correctly depicted with a gilt wreath round the neck – not a universal feature.

A Hamilton-Smith print of the capture of the Barrosa Eagle; published later than that of Dighton, it shows items of dress and insignia introduced after the battle, and it too must therefore be dismissed as an accurate representation of the 2/87th at Barrosa, or of Sgt. Masterson. The odd reversal of the sleeve chevrons is unexplained. Note that in both this and the Dighton print (left) Masterson is shown as a centre company sergeant armed with a pike.

By contrast, another contemporary print of the capture of the Barrosa Eagle depicts Masterson as a sergeant of the grenadier company and shows uniform details fairly accurately for that identification (note badges of rank on both sleeves, which were not introduced until c.1812 – cf. Plate C1 – and shoulder wings). It is unlikely that he cut his way through the mêlée with a sabre, however. The fallen British officer shown in the foreground may represent Ensign Keogh, who was bayoneted twice and killed during the attack on the Eagle guard.

PORTUGAL, 1813
1: Private, 18th Hussars
2: Corporal, 4th Royal Irish Dragoon Guards

A

TALAVERA, 1809
1: Corporal, Light Company, 1/88th Regt
2: Private of centre company, 2/87th Regt
3: Company officer, 2/87th Regt

B

BUSACO, BAROSSA AND TARIFA, 1810–11
1: Sergeant, Grenadier Company, 2/87th Regt
2: Drummer, 2/87th Regt
3: Private, 1/88th Regt

BADAJOZ AND SALAMANCA, 1812
1: Corporal of centre company, 1/88th Regt, Badajoz
2: Private & field officer, 1/88th Regt, Salamanca

D

SOUTH-EASTERN SPAIN, 1813
1: Captain, Grenadier Company, 2/27th Regt, Castalla
2: Captain, Light Company, 2/27th Regt, Alcoy
3: Sergeant, Grenadier Company, 1/27th Regt

E

VITTORIA, 1813
1: Corporal, 18th Hussars
2: Sergeant, Light Company, 2/87th Regt
3: Private, 1/88th Regt
4: Private, 3/27th Regt, marching order

F

WINTER DRESS, 1808–14
1: Officer, 1/88th Regt
2: Officer, 3/27th Regt
3: Sergeant, 1/88th Regt

G

INSIGNIA -
see text commentary for details

8

1

2

3

4

5

6
18
LD

7

9

Chappell ~ 02

H

In this part of the field 2,600 British in line were now facing 4,000 French in column. As the two bodies closed the first volleys of musketry were exchanged at a range of 60 paces, the concentrated fire of the British line cutting down the front ranks of the French columns and bringing them to a halt. As the 87th got to within 25 paces the enemy began to break, and Graham gave the order to charge. The 2/87th 'charged muskets' and dashed forward with cries of *'Faugh-a-Ballagh! Faugh-a-Ballagh!'* ('Clear the way!'). The commander of the French 2/8e Régiment de Ligne found himself 'In the midst of the most terrible bayonet fight I had ever seen … Every man was fighting for himself … the remnants of my battalion … gave way, and a further vigorous charge by the 87th British Regiment completed its overthrow'. Gough admitted, 'It was … a scene of most dreadful carnage'. The 8e de Ligne lost 700 men, its colonel and both battalion commanders. It also lost its Eagle standard, about which a desperate struggle raged until Sgt. Patrick Masterson seized it from the mortally wounded Sous-lieutenant Guillemain, crying, 'Bejabers, boys, I have the cuckoo!'

Having defeated the 8e de Ligne the 2/87th faced the incoming 45e de Ligne, and drove them off with musketry. Defeated, the entire French force marched away. Graham's 5,000 troops had defeated a force of 7,000 French, after inflicting over 2,000 casualties on them. He marched his tired men back into the Cadiz garrison on the same day.

When the news of Barrosa reached England the fortunes of the 2/87th began to look up. By an order of 18 April 1811 the Prince Regent proclaimed the regiment 'The 87th, or Prince of Wales's Own Irish', and ordered borne on its colours and appointments 'an Eagle with a wreath of Laurel, above the Harp, in addition to the arms of His Royal Highness', in commemoration of the battle. Gough was made brevet lieutenant-colonel, and Masterson was rewarded with a commission in the Royal York Light Infantry Volunteers – a slightly dubious reward, given that this was a regiment of Dutch turncoats and French deserters serving in the disease-ridden West Indies.

In October 1811 eight companies of the 2/87th were sent again to Tarifa, which was under threat from the French. Eventually the whole Anglo-Spanish force in Tarifa (which included the Irlanda Regiment) found themselves under siege. The 2/87th played a particularly distinguished part on the morning of 31 December, when 2,000 French grenadiers and light infantry attacked the position they were holding. The enemy, struggling through pelting rain and deep mud, approached the 2/87th only to be shot down by a hail of grape from artillery and devastating musketry. Above the roar of the battle could be heard the drums and fifes of the defenders playing 'Garryowen' and 'St Patrick's Day'. In half an hour the French lost over 200 men.

1812–14

On 5 January 1812 the French squelched away from Tarifa, and in August they gave up the siege of Cadiz altogether, whereupon the 2/87th began the long march north to rejoin Wellington's army. They joined its 4th Division near Madrid on 25 October, just in time to begin the retreat that followed Wellington's siege of Burgos. In foul weather

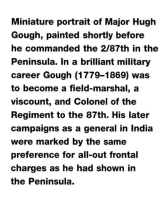

Miniature portrait of Major Hugh Gough, painted shortly before he commanded the 2/87th in the Peninsula. In a brilliant military career Gough (1779–1869) was to become a field-marshal, a viscount, and Colonel of the Regiment to the 87th. His later campaigns as a general in India were marked by the same preference for all-out frontal charges as he had shown in the Peninsula.

his army struggled back to Portugal, losing men to the French pursuit, sickness and desertion as the supply system and discipline broke down.

Over the winter of 1812/1813 the 2/87th, like the rest of Wellington's regiments, were restored in numbers, equipment and health until, in mid-May, they marched into Spain once more, driving the French before them until they came to Vittoria. There, on 21 June 1813, the 2/87th served in Colville's brigade, formed on the left of Wellington's main body. At midday the bugles sounded the 'advance'; the 2/87th crossed the Zadorra river and moved under heavy fire against the village of Margarita, sweeping the French from it with a charge that also pushed the enemy out of the village of Hermandad half a mile away. Gough wrote next day that 'the officers and men ... really have proved themselves heroes... I regret to tell you my loss was enormous ...' – in fact, 88 dead and 166 wounded from a strength of 637 men.

The Allied army pushed on against crumbling French resistance until they found themselves in the midst of that magnificent prize, the abandoned enemy baggage train. The frenzy of looting that followed put a virtual end to the battle and let slip the chance of a total victory for Wellington. Gough claimed, 'Some of my fellows have made fortunes, but much less than the old soldiers of other Corps ... one of my Sergeants got the Batonner (Truncheon) of Marshall Jourdain ... The young rascal has taken off the two Gold Eagles on either end, which he pretends he has lost.'

For the 2/87th the months that followed Vittoria involved them in a great deal of marching and countermarching but no fighting until 10 November, when Wellington forced a passage of the River Nivelle. On that day the battalion lost 216 men out of a total of 386 who went into action. Reduced to a mere detachment, the 2/87th were not strong enough to fight again as a battalion until the battle of Orthez on 27 February 1814 when, as part of the 3rd Division, they had to endure a two-hour bombardment by the French artillery before being ordered into an attack on the left of the enemy position. The fighting was most severe at this point, and the 2/87th lost 109 out of a strength of 350 men.

By the time of the advance on Toulouse the 2/87th were once more marching with the 3rd Division – but only 450 strong, a shadow of the battalion of former years. In the battle of 10 April the 2/87th provided 'fire support', shooting at the enemy from the cover of loop-holed houses; even so, they lost 27 men.

Rank-and-file jacket of a grenadier company private of the 87th (Prince of Wales's Irish) Regt, c.1808 or earlier. Thought never to have been issued, it lacks the fringes that would have been added to the wings by regimental tailors. The 'dull green' facings are displayed at the collar, cuffs and shoulder straps. The wings are red, with the regulation edge and six darts of regimental lace – see Plate H2; this also edges shoulder straps and the white turnbacks. Note that the loops are set points-down on the cuffs, points-up on the horizontal false pockets. The pewter buttons bear the Prince of Wales' plumes and motto scroll, over a harp, over '87'. This was the type of jacket worn by the rank-and-file of the 2/87th on their arrival in Lisbon in 1809. (Royal Irish Fusiliers Museum)

With the abdication of Napoleon the 2nd Bn of the 87th, The Prince of Wales's Own Irish Regiment of Foot (the 'Faugh-a-Ballaghs', or the 'Eagle Catchers') sailed for Ireland and thence to England. They guarded American prisoners-of-war at Dartmoor before moving to Guernsey, where Sir John Doyle was still governor. There the battalion remained through the year of Waterloo, returning to England only to be disbanded in January 1817. In its short existence it had won for its regiment the battle honours PENINSULA, TALAVERA, BARROSA, TARIFA, VITTORIA, NIVELLE, ORTHES and TOULOUSE.

Part of General Baron Lejeune's painting of the battle of Chiclana (as the French called Barrosa), March 1811. Seen in the background is the port of Cadiz, while the tower of Barrosa is visible on the high ground to the left. A talented soldier-artist, Lejeune served in the Peninsula and later painted several spirited canvases of episodes during his years spent following Napoleon's star.

THE 88th (THE CONNAUGHT RANGERS) REGIMENT OF FOOT

This regiment was another of those raised as a consequence of the outbreak of war between England and revolutionary France. A Colonel de Burgh raised it, mainly in the province of Connaught, under a commission dated 25 September 1793. Even before receiving its number as a regiment of the Line it became known as the Connaught Rangers, 'Rangers' being a favourite title for provincial levies at that time. Most of the officers were Irishmen, and all had raised men for rank – i.e. receiving commissions according to the recruits they brought in. The regiment moved to England, was numbered 88th, and received its first stand of colours and the first of many commanding officers.

In 1794 it was part of the disastrous campaign in Holland under the 'Grand Old Duke of York'. Returning to England with 543 men sick out of 773, it was taken over by a new commanding officer, Lt.Col. William Carr Beresford, the giant Anglo-Irishman who was to become a general, a marshal in the Portuguese Army, and a viscount. He rebuilt the Connaught Rangers and embarked with them on a series of campaigns that took them to the West Indies, Jersey, India, Egypt and South America before returning to England in 1807. By this time Beresford had left the regiment for higher command, but their paths were to cross again in the Peninsula.

In 1804 a 2nd Bn to the Connaught Rangers was raised under the Additional Forces Act. Its first commanding officer was Lt.Col. John Alexander Wallace, an officer who would later command the 1/88th in the Peninsula. After being stationed in Scotland and England the

Field-Marshal William Carr Beresford, 1st Viscount Beresford, from a portrait made in old age. Having commanded the Connaught Rangers, he later became Colonel of the Regiment. Perhaps his greatest achievement in the Peninsula was his reorganisation and training of the Portuguese Army.

2/88th returned to Ireland in 1807, being stationed in Connaught where many recruits were obtained from Irish Militia regiments.

1809

The 1st Bn of the Connaught Rangers received orders for the Peninsula and sailed on 28 December 1808, in the same convoy of ships as the 2/87th, and on landing were brigaded with that battalion. Both units suffered the trial of the 'barefoot' pursuit of the French under Beresford; both were caught napping by the enemy before Talavera, and earned the wrath of Wellington. But unlike the 2/87th, the Connaught Rangers were not sent to kick their heels in Cadiz. They remained part of the 3rd Division, later to be nicknamed the 'Fighting Division' for reasons that will become apparent.

In September 1809 Lt.Col. Wallace arrived from England with a draft of men from the 2nd Bn and took over command of the 1/88th. He set about improving the drill and discipline of his new command, and had made great progress when Maj.Gen. Thomas Picton arrived to take over command of the division. Picton, a Welshman, declared his aversion to the 1/88th from the start. Having reviewed a faultless demonstration of drill by his division, he was about to depart when two stragglers of the Connaught Rangers were brought in under arrest. They had stolen a goat whilst absent from their regiment, and Picton immediately convened a drumhead court martial and saw the men flogged in the presence of the entire division. The general then turned to the 1/88th and declared that they were better known as 'Irish robbers and common footpads than as Connaught Rangers'; he went on to make further intemperate and scathing remarks about their country and their religion. The incident was to sour the relationship between Picton and the Connaught Rangers, for although the regiment went on to prove themselves one of the best, if not the best in Wellington's army, Picton continued to discriminate against the unit in various ways, including recommending none of its officers for promotion.

1810

From this point onwards the 1/88th were to fight in all the great battles of Wellington's main army, and to fight with great distinction. The first occasion was at Busaco, where on the night of 26 September 1810 a combined Anglo-Portuguese army took up positions on the ridge with the 3rd Division at the centre of the line. As dawn broke the following morning the light troops of both armies began to stalk each other in the mists that cloaked the slopes, and as their musketry crackled the approach of the French infantry columns could be heard. One of them, numbering more than 6,000 men, began to climb towards a gully where it threatened to break into the British line between the Connaught Rangers and the 1/45th. As the fog cleared the fire of the mass of light troops preceding the French column began to inflict casualties in the ranks of the Connaught Rangers. As one history tersely puts it, 'General Picton was not within reach at the instant, and the 88th was without orders'.

Colonel Wallace, seizing the initiative, shouted above the din of battle to his men: 'Be cool, be steady, but above all, pay attention to my word of command – you know it well. You see how these Frenchmen press on; let them do so; when they reach a little near us I will order you to advance to that mount – look at it lest you might mistake what I say. Now mind what I tell you; when you arrive at that spot, I will charge, and I have now only to add, the rest must be done by yourselves – press them to the muzzle, I say. CONNAUGHT RANGERS! Press on the rascals!'

Wallace's address was received in silence. He then marched his battalion nearer the 1/45th, detached three companies to deal with some French light troops who had taken a knoll in the crest, and formed the rest into line to open fire against the flank of the ascending French column. (During this movement the Connaught Rangers had been subjected to what would today be called 'friendly fire' from the green 8th Portuguese Infantry. Lieutenant Fitzpatrick, sent to point out the error, had only time to wave his hat and cry out 'Vamos commarades!' before he received one bullet from the French and another from the Portuguese.) Wallace then dismounted, and with two fellow officers ran forward to charge the advancing French. Through the smoke he could be seen parrying and thrusting, and shouting to his men to press on. Thus began a desperate bayonet charge by the Connaught Rangers in which they drove the numerically superior French column back down the slopes of the ridge before forming line at the bottom; behind them lay 200 French dead and many more wounded. Their charge had broken the enemy assault on the centre of Wellington's line and, with the repulse of the French elsewhere, the day was his. The French lost 4,600 men at Busaco, the British 626 and the Portuguese the same. The Connaught Rangers lost 134 officers and men, more than any other Allied battalion.

A contemporary print of the battle of Busaco, showing the 1/88th, on the left of the picture, about to drive the columns of French back down the ridge.

'Ciudad Rodrigo on the morning after the storm'. The breach through which Lieutenant Mackie led the 'forlorn hope' of the Connaught Rangers may be seen above the cannon, half right. Before the assault Picton called out: 'Rangers of Connaught! It is not my intention to expend powder this evening. We will do the business with the cold iron!' His exhortation is reported to have been greeted with a 'vehement cheer'.

Wellington himself, who had seen the action of the Connaught Rangers, rode up to say to Wallace, 'I never saw a more gallant charge than that just now made by your regiment'. In his public dispatches he mentioned Col. Wallace, the 1/88th and Capt. Dansey of the regiment. Marshal Beresford, by now colonel of the Connaught Rangers, also rode up to congratulate Wallace and to call out to older soldiers whom he recognised. Eventually Picton appeared, but he was not 'received with cordiality'; a wag called Cooney cried out, 'Where were you this morning? Are we the Connaught Footpads now?' He risked a flogging, but he probably spoke for all who had endured Picton's insults at the divisional review.

As the wounded were being tended an officer of the Connaught Rangers records having spoken to men in the uniform of Napoleon's Régiment Irlandais, or the Irish Brigade as he called them, none of whom appeared to be Irishmen. Two battalions of the Irlandais were certainly present at Busaco, but remained in reserve with the rest of the French 3rd Division. They may have contributed light troops to reinforce those of the attacking formations, as the French skirmishers at Busaco were noted as being in greater numbers than usual.

1811

After Busaco Wellington withdrew his forces within the prepared defences of the Lines of Torres Vedras, leaving the pursuing French to starve in a region that had been stripped of most that was needed to sustain an army. By the spring of 1811 they began to evacuate Portugal, harried by the Allied pursuit into Spain where, in May, they turned to fight. Their approach lay through the village of Fuentes de Oñoro, about which Wellington disposed his forces for battle.

The battle began on 3 May when five French infantry divisions advanced on Fuentes de Oñoro, where bloody and confused fighting took place in the streets. The village was taken and retaken, until nightfall brought an end to the slaughter with each side holding part of it, the British still clinging on in the upper part around the church. The following day saw a lull in the fighting as the French reconnoitred the Allied positions and the Allies strengthened their defences.

The 5th dawned to the roar of French artillery as 5,000 of their infantry stormed and turned Wellington's right, throwing themselves once more against the battered hovels and up the sloping alleys. At 12.30pm a crisis was reached, and Wellington ordered forward four British battalions and two Portuguese infantry regiments; in the van were the Connaught Rangers. An officer commanding its leading

company takes up the story: 'This battalion advanced with fixed bayonets in column of sections, left in front, in double quick time, their firelocks at the trail … There was no noise or talking in the ranks; the men stepped together at a smart trot, as if on parade, headed by [Colonel Wallace] … we came within sight of the French 9th Regiment [9e Régiment Léger] … I turned round to look at the men of my company; they gave me a cheer that a lapse of many years has not made me forget, and I thought that moment was the proudest of my life.'

The Connaught Rangers drove straight down into the French with the bayonet, column to column, their attack gathering momentum as those who had fought the French all morning joined the advancing Irish to drive the enemy from the village; 150 grenadiers, trapped in a blind alley, were shot and bayoneted to a man. As soon as Fuentes de Oñoro had been cleared the Connaught Rangers took post behind its ruined walls. When darkness fell the village was again put in a state of defence, but the battle was over; exchanges of artillery and the bickering of light troops continued until the French eventually marched away. Wellington later mentioned Col. Wallace and his battalion in dispatches, noting the important part they had played in the fighting.

(The Régiment Irlandais, by then down to one battalion, was also present at Fuentes de Oñoro, but was not committed to the fighting. In August 1811 its title was changed to '3rd Foreign Regiment (Irish)', the renaming reflecting how few Irishmen remained in its ranks by then.)

By June 1811 the Connaught Rangers found themselves part of the force besieging the fortress of Badajoz, but the investment was abandoned when Wellington moved against the northern fortress of Ciudad Rodrigo. It was at this time that the 2/88th was drafted into the 1st Battalion. The 2nd Bn had sailed for the Peninsula in the summer of 1809, joining first the garrison of Gibraltar and then that of Cadiz. In August 1810 the 2/88th moved to Lisbon and in March 1811 joined the 3rd Division. After the battle of Fuentes de Oñoro it was decided to draft the private soldiers of the 2/88th into the 1/88th whilst its officers and non-commissioned officers were to return to Ireland to recruit new drafts for the 1st Battalion.

On 25 September 1811 the Connaught Rangers fought in the 'combat' of El Bodon, in which a masterly fighting withdrawal of eight miles was conducted while under attack by a large force of French cavalry and artillery.

1812

Thereafter time passed quietly for the battalion until January 1812, when the 1/88th was ordered into the trenches around the strategic border fortress of Ciudad Rodrigo. By 19 January two breaches had been battered into the fortress' walls, and the 3rd Division was ordered to storm the larger one. The 'honour' of finding the 'forlorn hope' – the party to lead the stormers, whose hopes of survival were slim – went to the Connaught Rangers: 20 men led by Lieutenant Mackie. Despite

Violent, intemperate and profane were among the words used to describe Maj.Gen. Thomas Picton (1758–1815), who was 52 when Wellington requested that he be sent out to the Peninsula to command his 3rd Division. In his dealings with the Connaught Rangers the Welshman declared from the very start his dislike of Irishmen in general and Irish Catholics in particular. His outbursts were resented by the officers he vilified (their attempts to gain redress are a matter of record); but he must have been positively loathed by the rank-and-file of the Connaught Rangers, some of whom risked flogging or worse to be insubordinate to him in front of their comrades. The formal portrait shows him in the uniform of a lieutenant-general, the rank to which he was promoted in 1813, the year he was knighted. The less well known drawing shows him in the civilian hat and coat that he customarily wore in the field.

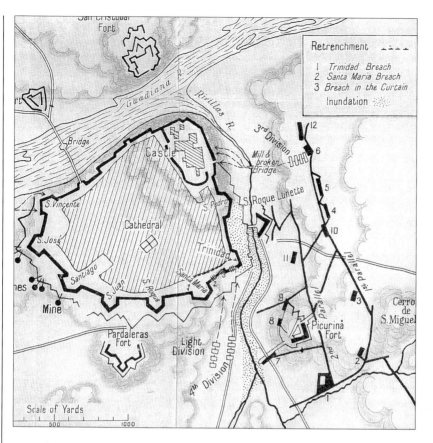

Badajoz, 6 April 1812, showing the location of the breaches, and those of the 'escalade' assaults (3rd Division, top right, and Walker's Brigade, left). At the castle the men of the 3rd Division were slaughtered for over an hour until two ladders were successfully mounted against its wall and a lodgement was secured. Again, Lt.Mackie of the 88th led one of these parties; Capt. Oates of the same regiment had previously led a successful assault on Fort Picurina (bottom right).

Within the map:
Retrenchment
1 *Trinidad Breach*
2 *Santa Maria Breach*
3 *Breach in the Curtain*
Inundation

murderous musketry, cannon fire, and the firing of a huge mine that alone killed over 150 of the stormers, Mackie led the survivors to the citadel to take its surrender. The fortress was then sacked. (By the conventions of the time it was understood that once the walls of a place under siege had been breached, the opportunity existed for the garrison to surrender honourably. If they chose not to do so, thus forcing the besiegers to face the inevitably bloody cost of an actual assault, then storming parties had the right to put them to the sword and sack their fortress in search of the spoils of war.) The 1/88th were again mentioned in Wellington's dispatches.

With one border fortress in his hands Wellington turned to the other, Badajoz, and once again the men of the 3rd Division found themselves digging trenches before its walls. On the night of 25 March a first attempt was made to storm the breaches thus far opened. It was repulsed with terrible casualties, but Capt. Oates of the Connaught Rangers led a party that captured Fort Picurina, one of the outlying defence works. By the night of 6 April further breaching had taken place and Wellington's men were ready to try again. In a bloody and desperate battle all of the stormers of the breaches were repulsed, but three attacks made by escalade (ladders) succeeded. One of these was made by the battalions of Picton's 3rd Division, and the Connaught Rangers played their part in the hours of fighting that ensued before sufficient numbers to secure its capture had scaled the walls of the castle of Badajoz. Their success was the turning point, and the defence was steadily overcome as the number of stormers within the walls of Badajoz grew. With the defeat of the French garrison the inevitable plundering began, accompanied by drunken violence and rape. At Badajoz the pillaging was on a scale commensurate with the casualties suffered in its capture: 4,670 of the attackers had been killed or wounded, and Badajoz was made to pay.

The Connaught Rangers next saw action at Salamanca on 2 July when, at 5pm, after a day of marching and manoeuvring in parallel with the French, Wellington ordered the 3rd Division to advance to take the heights and guns to its front. Colours were uncased, bayonets fixed, muskets primed and loaded, and the division stepped off with the Connaught Rangers in the first column. The French immediately opened fire with artillery, and their light troops peppered the advancing formation as it deployed from column into line whilst on the march. A charge by French cavalry was beaten off, and the line of the 3rd Division came under fire as it closed with the enemy on the crest of the ridge (these included the 1er, 62e and 101e Régiments de Ligne.) At this point the officer commanding the Connaught Rangers was shot dead and his body, caught by a foot jammed in a stirrup, was dragged in front of the battalion by his horse. The effect on the Connaught Rangers was seen by Gen. Pakenham, who shouted to the brigade commander, 'Let them loose!' Instantly the line leapt forward, its impact shattering the French column and driving it back on itself as both sides fought with bayonet and bullet.

With the air thick with smoke little could be seen of the battle, but from time to time the hammering of hooves and the jingle of harness indicated that cavalry was near. One such warning proved to be the brigade of British heavy cavalry of Gen. Le Marchant, coming on at a canter; they passed through the infantry of the 3rd Division and 'swept away' the enemy infantry to complete the destruction of the French left wing. Elsewhere on the field of Salamanca the story was the same; the French were in retreat, having lost over 14,000 men, killed, wounded and prisoners, two Eagles, six other colours and 20 guns. It was the Connaught Rangers who captured the 'Jingling Johnnie' or *Schellenbaum* of the French 101e de Ligne's *tête de colonne*.

After the battle the Connaught Rangers marched on to Madrid, where it stayed until Wellington began his withdrawal back to Portugal. The horrors of the retreat from Burgos have been mentioned above; the Connaught Rangers suffered these in full measure.

1813–14

Reinforced, re-equipped and rested, the battalion once again advanced into Spain in May 1813, fighting in the battle of Vittoria the following month. On the day of the battle the Connaught Rangers were once again harangued by Picton (back in command of the 3rd Division after sick leave) when he found them halted at the orders of their brigade commander. The notoriously foul-mouthed Welshman used 'some harsh expressions' before the situation was explained by the brigade commander (he was later forced to pen an apology for his outburst). As the 1/88th moved off Picton called to them, 'Rangers of Connaught, drive those French rascals into the village and out of the village – you are the lads that know how to do it!' Drive they did, the French never stopping to cross bayonets with them; but the 1/88th still suffered 200 casualties in the battle.

In July the battalion fought as part of the force covering the siege of Pamplona, after which it operated in the Pyrenees until November and December, supporting the storming of the French defences on

At Salamanca in 1812 the Connaught Rangers captured the 'Jingling Johnnie' or *Schellen-baum* – a peculiar trophy of a kind which can be traced back to Austria's wars with the Turks – from the *tête de colonne* of the French 101e de Ligne. This late 19th-century photograph shows the Peninsular War colours of the 1/88th and the 'Jingling Johnnie'. Working a crank agitated the upper part of the instrument, causing the dozens of small bells to sound. This trophy was carried by the bands of the Connaught Rangers from 1812 until the regiment was disbanded in the early 1920s.

In 1818, Col. Wallace obtained permission to issue medals to those Connaught Rangers who were veterans of the Peninsula. His 'Regimental Order of Merit' was in three classes, all in silver. The first class award, in the shape of a Maltese Cross, was awarded to those who had fought in 12 actions. The second and third class awards were medals, given for participation in from seven to 11 actions, and six or fewer actions, respectively. The expense of the medals was borne by the officers of the 88th.

The obverse and reverse of a gold medal for valour awarded to Private John Murphy of the Connaught Rangers for his bravery at Badajoz. Murphy lived long enough to claim the Military General Service Medal, authorised in 1847, qualifying for 12 clasps. There is no record of Murphy ever receiving the Regimental Order of Merit, reserved for 'past service and good conduct'; the assumption must therefore be that although his bravery and stamina were irreproachable, his conduct when out of battle was not.

the rivers Nivelle and Nive before going into winter quarters.

At the battle of Orthez in February 1814 the Connaught Rangers suffered 269 casualties in the attack of the 3rd Division on the French positions – losses so severe that the battalion was taken out of the line until 13 March. At the battle of Toulouse in April only three companies could take the field; in supporting two battalions engaged with superior numbers of the enemy, these companies suffered 86 casualties.

When the fighting in southern France came to an end the Connaught Rangers were ordered to embark for America where a war was still being waged. The 1st Bn of the 88th Regiment of Foot had served Wellington in Portugal, Spain and France for just over five years, most of the time in the 3rd 'Fighting Division'; the 2nd Bn had served in Portugal and Spain for two years. The records show that in that time 36 officers of the battalion lost their lives – no record exists of the exact number of rank-and-file of the Connaught Rangers who fell. When the time came for the award of battle honours for the war, those for the Connaught Rangers were: PENINSULA, TALAVERA, BUSACO, FUENTES D'ONOR, CUIDAD RODRIGO [sic], SALAMANCA, ORTHES, TOULOUSE, BADAJOZ, VITTORIA and NIVELLE.

SELECT BIBLIOGRAPHY

M.Cunliffe, *The Royal Irish Fusiliers 1793–1950*, London (1952)

William Grattan, *Adventures with the Connaught Rangers 1809–1814*, London (reprint 1989)

Historical Records of the British Army: The 4th Royal Irish Dragoon Guards, London (1847)

Lt.Col. H.F.N.Jourdain, *The Connaught Rangers*, London (1924)

Col. H.Malet, *Memoirs of the 18th Hussars*, London (1907)

Sir Charles Oman, *A History of the Peninsular War* (7 vols), Greenhill Books reprint (1995)

W.Copeland Trimble, *The 27th Inniskilling Regiment*, London (1876)

THE PLATES

A: PORTUGAL, 1813
A1: Private, 18th Hussars
A2: Corporal, 4th Royal Irish Dragoon Guards

In April 1813 the 18th Hussars had recently arrived in Lisbon whilst the 4th Dragoon Guards were marching there for embarkation and the journey back to England. The paths of the two regiments may have crossed in the manner depicted, which shows a mounted dragoon of the 18th Hussars 'looking down on' a corporal of the 4th Dragoon Guards.

Review order for 'Drogheda's Cossacks' in early 1813 was recorded thus: 'White leather pantaloons, white leather sword and pouch belts. Regimental fur caps, cap lines and feather. Regimental jacket, hussar sash with three rows of knots in front – regimental sabretache – pelisses slung – plain bridles and furniture well cleaned.' The white facings of the regiment are noticeable on the collar and cuffs of the hussar jacket and the fleece trim of the pelisse, and also on the 'Vandyke' surround of the shabraque.

The 4th Royal Irish Dragoon Guards handed over their horses to other regiments before marching to Lisbon, carrying their arms and equipment as best they could. The corporal depicted has rolled his cloak around his valise and sword, and hitched up his sabretache to make his load manageable. He has also removed the spurs from his jackboots, but his outfit is ill-suited for footslogging. Note that the '1812' uniforms for heavy cavalry had not yet reached the 4th Dragoon Guards by this date.

B: TALAVERA, 1809
B1: Corporal, Light Company, 1/88th Regiment
B2: Private of a centre company, 2/87th Regiment
B3: Company officer, 2/87th Regiment

The corporal of the Connaught Rangers (B1) is kneeling ready to take a shot while skirmishing. Note his shako details: the light company tuft, the bugle-horn badge on the cockade, and the regimental number stamped into his cap-plate. The yellow regimental 'facings' are visible at collar and cuffs, and in the backing to the chevrons of his badge of rank; note the flank company 'wings' at his shoulders, and his regimental 'breastplate' – the buckle plate of his bayonet cross belt. His musket or 'firelock' is the India Pattern. His knapsack is painted the facing colour of his regiment, and has a blanket rolled

Officer's shoulder belt plate of the 87th (Prince of Wales's Irish) Regt, c.1800–11. The plate is silver with the harp and beaded edge in gilt. After Barrosa the eagle was incorporated into the design.

above it, with his 60-round cartridge pouch below. His 'marching order' is completed by a haversack and a blue-painted water canteen, both of which hang at his left side.

To the rear a private of the 2/87th (B2) stands at the 'charge muskets, breast high' position, which would be adopted by men in the rear of the two ranks of the line formation. He too is in marching order, but note the shako tuft and epaulette tufts denoting a man of one of the battalion's centre companies. Note also the 'dull green' of his regimental facings and knapsack. Both figures wear the woollen 'overalls' of the time (which buttoned up the side), and black woollen gaiters.

In the background, junior officers of the 2/87th (B3) and the Spanish Regiment Irlanda (B4) salute one another. Note the colour distinction between the scarlet coat of the officer and the red jackets of the soldiers. The coat of the Irish-Spaniard is the sky-blue of all the Irish regiments in the service of Spain, with the yellow facings of the Irlanda. Spain's Irish regiments were said to be some of the most reliable in its army.

Rank-and-file shoulder belt plate of the 87th (Prince of Wales's Irish) Regiment prior to 1811. It is brass, and of the oval-shaped 'Ordnance' pattern, with the design engraved. After Barrosa a new design incorporated the eagle, the numerals 'LXXXVII', and the legend 'PRINCE.OF.WALES'S.OWN.IRISH.REGT.'

C: BUSACO, BAROSSA and TARIFA, 1810–11
C1: Sergeant, Grenadier Company, 2/87th Regiment
C2: Drummer, 2/87th Regiment
C3: Private, 1/88th Regiment

The Eagle standard of the French 8e de Ligne taken at Barossa by Sgt. Masterson of the 2/87th was the first to be captured by a British regiment during the Napoleonic War; here it is being admired by a grenadier sergeant (**C1**) and a drummer (**C2**) after the battle. Note the sergeant's dress distinctions, which include a well-cut jacket of scarlet cloth, plain white lace, a worsted sash with a line of facing colour woven into it, a 1796 pattern infantry sword, and the badges of rank on the right sleeve only at this date. As a member of the battalion's grenadier company he wears flank company 'wings', and an all-white feather hackle in his shako. The drummer wears 'reversed colours' – a coat of the regimental facing colour, 'dull green', faced with red. It is decorated with wings and many yards of drummer's lace. His drum is painted in the regiment's facing colour and embellished with the crown and cipher of King George III and the regimental title. This is the dress worn by the fifes and drums of the 2/87th when they played at the defence of Tarifa. Note the sergeant's overalls, and the breeches and gaiters of the drummer.

In the background, a private of the Connaught Rangers (**C3**) is taking prisoner a *voltigeur* from the light infantry company of the French Régiment Irlandais at Busaco, 1810. At this time a 'Captain Hussey from Sligo', a Captain Reilly and a Sergeant-Major Dwyer were reported to be doing the rounds of British prisoners-of-war to enlist men for Napoleon's 'Irish Brigade'. They sought Irishmen and Scotsmen, but took English as well; but the recruiting effort was only marginally successful, since it is known that many Poles served in the Régiment Irlandais, their drum-major was Prussian, and a return of 1812 showed 21 different nationalities including five men from the United States, but only 86 Irishmen.

D: BADAJOZ and SALAMANCA, 1812
D1: Corporal of a centre company, 1/88th Regiment, Badajoz
D2: Private and field officer, 1/88th Regiment, Salamanca

In his *Adventures with the Connaught Rangers*, Lieutenant William Grattan has left us several descriptions of the dress of his battalion in the Peninsula. Before they climbed the scaling ladders against the walls of the castle of Badajoz he noted: 'the soldiers, unencumbered with their knapsacks... their stocks off ... their shirt-collars unbuttoned ... their trousers tucked up to the knee ... their tattered jackets, so

ABOVE **The Barrosa Eagle was one of those decorated with a gold wreath of laurels, presented by the city of Paris to the regiments involved in the Austerlitz campaign (the eagles themselves were of bronze.) This image shows how the eagles so decorated should have looked.**
LEFT **A drawing by Lieutenant Pym of the 2/87th showing the eagle of the 8e de Ligne after its capture. Note that the thunderbolt is missing from the beneath the right foot, and that several of the leaves from the wreath have been 'souvenired'; cf Plate C.**

worn out as to render the regiment they belonged to barely recognisable … their huge whiskers and bronzed faces, which several hard-fought campaigns had changed from their natural hue …' There are also references to men pulling their cartridge pouches round to the front and securing them there by using their musket slings as waist belts. Figure **D1** depicts one of the stormers after the taking of the city. He has replaced his shako (if he ever had one) with one of the many patterns of 'night' cap worn at the time. His shabby red jacket and cotton drill trousers reflect Grattan's description, as does his minimal equipment – which includes a haversack stuffed with loot. He has replaced his canteen with a bottle of brandy to 'refresh' himself as he continues his search.

In the background, a soldier of the Connaught Rangers is depicted offering the 'Jingling Johnnie' or *Schellenbaum* which the battalion captured from the *tête de colonne* of the French 101e de Ligne to a mounted field officer of his regiment. Note the knapsack's painted badge: the regimental name in white on a dark circlet, around '88' on a red disc.

The jacket of Captain Charles Parsons, mortally wounded at Alcoy, Spain, in March 1813 whilst commanding the light company of the 2/27th (Enniskillen) Regiment. The jacket is of scarlet cloth and the facings are light buff; the bugle-horn badges that should have been worn on the wings and turnbacks have been removed. When Capt. Parsons' jacket was discovered in 1942 it had with it a light infantry sash, a waterbottle, a haversack and a dirk – see Plate E2.

E: SOUTH-EASTERN SPAIN, 1813
E1: Captain, Grenadier Company, 2/27th Regiment, Castalla
E2: Captain, Light Company, 2/27th Regiment, Alcoy
E3: Sergeant, Grenadier Company, 1/27th Regiment
The 1st and 2nd Battalions of the 27th (Enniskillen) Regiment landed at Alicante in December 1812 and formed part of an Allied force operating in this region. They were at the battle

in which three dice were rolled against a stop – in this case a knapsack – to make doubles amounting to ten or better.) Figure **F1** depicts Corporal Fox, 18th Hussars, unscrewing the ends of the baton of Marshal Jourdan – he probably thought the shaft was worthless. Figure **F2** depicts a sergeant of the Light Company of the 2/87th, the battalion which later 'acquired' the baton and got the credit for passing it on to Wellington (who sent it to the Prince Regent, who, in return, promoted Wellington Britain's first Field-Marshal, sending him a baton based on Jourdan's but designed by himself). Figure **F3** depicts a private of the Connaught Rangers, the 'cully' running the game. All take their ease in various states of relaxed dress; note the forage cap of the hussar and the 'nightcap' of the sergeant. In the background, **F4** is a private of the 3/27th, 'The Young Enniskillens', in marching order. Note his India Pattern musket and bayonet, cartridge pouch, haversack, canteen, blanket, mess tin and knapsack. Note also the markings on his canteen and

LEFT **The rank-and-file shoulder belt plate of the 27th (Enniskillen) Regt at the time of the Peninsular War. Cast in brass, it differed from the oval 'Ordnance' pattern.**

BELOW **Rank-and-file shako plate of the 27th (Enniskillen) Regt, 1811–16, worn with the 'Belgique' or 'Wellington' shako. Although authorised in 1811 this headdress did not come into use in the Peninsula until the last months of the war. See Plate E1 for officer's bi-metal version.**

of Castalla on 13 April 1813 when, before the fighting started, a Captain Waldron of the 2/27th fought a duel with a French grenadier officer. Figure **E1** depicts Waldron – himself a grenadier – about to deliver the 'coup de grace' on that occasion. He wears the shako and jacket ordered for infantry officers in 1811, pantaloons and boots. Note the shako plume and wings of a grenadier officer, his 1803 pattern infantry sabre (regulation for flank company officers, but also carried by many other officers), and the buff facings of the 27th.

In March 1813 Captain Parsons of the light company of the 2/27th lost his life in an action at Alcoy. Parts of his uniform and equipment have been preserved to this day, and figure **E2** shows these. Note his light infantry sash, haversack, flask and dirk; and also the light company bugle-horn badges on his wings and his jacket turnbacks. He carries his 1803 pattern sabre from a shoulder belt, which has a plate displaying the castle of Enniskillen.

Figure **E3** depicts a sergeant of the grenadier company of the 1/27th in 1813. He wears the old 'stovepipe' shako with the white hackle of a grenadier, a scarlet sergeant's jacket with grenadiers' wings and badges of rank (worn on both sleeves), white linen trousers, and a sergeant's worsted sash with a band of the regiment's facing colour. He is armed with a 1796 pattern sword and a seven-foot pike.

F: VITTORIA, 1813
F1: Corporal, 18th Hussars
F2: Sergeant, Light Company, 2/87th Regiment
F3: Private, 1/88th Regiment
F4: Private, 3/27th Regiment, marching order
Four of the five regiments featured in this title were represented at the battle of Vittoria. This plate depicts a scene after the battle when the plunder of the French baggage train was being divided and enjoyed. Three figures in the foreground are gambling with their newfound riches. (The game is 'Passage',

knapsack (and also on the knapsack being used as a gambling aid in the foreground). Compare the facings of the four regiments: white for 'Drogheda's', buff for the 27th, 'dull green' for the 87th and yellow for the Connaught Rangers.

G: WINTER DRESS, 1808–14
G1: Officer, 1/88th Regiment
G2: Officer, 3/27th Regiment
G3: Sergeant, 1/88th Regiment

In matters of officers' dress in the Peninsula, William Grattan of the 1/88th recorded that 'scarcely any two officers were dressed alike! Some with grey braided coats, others with brown; some again liked blue; while many from choice, or perhaps necessity, stuck to the "old red rag". Overalls, of all things, were in vogue, and the comical appearance of a number of infantry officers loaded with leather bottoms – and huge chains suspended from side buttons, like a parcel of dragoons, was amusing enough. Quantities of hair … a pair of mustachios, and screw brass spurs, were essential to a first-rate "Count" … the cut-down hat, exactly a [hand] span in height, was another "rage"; this burlesque on a "chapeau" was usually topped by some extraordinary-looking feather …'

Figure **G1** depicts the dress described by Grattan. Worn over it all is a 'boat cloak', a garment taken on campaign by most officers. Note his 'old red rag' of a regimental coat, 1796 pattern infantry sword, belt and plate, and sash.

In 1812 a greatcoat was authorised for infantry officers, to be of the same colour as those of the rank-and-file – grey. Figure **G2** depicts a junior officer of the 3/27th wearing such a coat in 1814; note that it is double-breasted, and lined with material of regimental facing colour. Figure **G3** depicts a sergeant of the Connaught Rangers in the rank-and-file greatcoat, 1808; sergeants' coats were modified by having collar and cuffs in the facing colour.

H: INSIGNIA

In common with all line infantry regiments, those reviewed in this title each had a distinctive pattern of 'lace' – in reality, white braid with coloured 'worms' or lines woven into it. This was sewn to the coats of privates and corporals, also in a distinctive manner. **H1** is that for the 27th (Enniskillen) Regiment, the 'loops' set on square and at equal distance. **H2** is that for the 87th (Prince of Wales's Own Irish) Regiment, set on with pointed ends and in pairs. **H3** is that for the 88th (Connaught Rangers) Regiment, also with pointed ends and in pairs. Note in each case the patterns of regimental buttons.

H4 and **H5** are two patterns of 'turnback' ornaments worn on the jackets of officers of the 27th – see Plate E – both featuring the castle of Enniskillen. **H6** is the silver ball button worn by officers of the 18th Light Dragoons (Hussars) in the Peninsula. **H7** is the shoulder belt plate of the rank-and-file of the Connaught Rangers.

H8 is taken from a silhouette made in 1807 of an officer of the light company of one of the battalions of the 87th. Note the details of his shako, plume and badge; his wing, shoulder belt plate, and light infantry sash. At this date flank companies seem to have worn false queue ribbons on the back of the collar, with a pigtail turned up under the shako.

Two regiments not mentioned in the text are the 'Royal Irish corps of Waggoners', which Wellesley took to Portugal

The dress of the British infantry officer for most of the Peninsular War was either the rather impractical regulation uniform or the 'improvisations' described by officers such as Grattan of the Connaught Rangers. The uniform ordered in December 1811 was much more suited to campaigning, with a shako in place of the bicorn hat, a shortened jacket in place of the long-tailed coat, grey overalls or trousers, and the caped greatcoat shown in this Hamilton-Smith print and in Plate G2.

with him in 1808; and the 2/89th Regiment, which was one of those garrisoning Gibraltar. The first seems to have been broken up soon after landing. The 89th was one of those regiments that chose not to have a title proclaiming it to be Irish. In October 1810 the 2/89th formed part of a force that sailed from Gibraltar and landed on the coast of south-eastern Spain at Fuengirola. Due to the ineptitude of the officer leading the force, 40 men of the 2/89th were killed and over 200 made prisoner. **H9** depicts a private of this unfortunate battalion in 1810; note the regiment's black facings, regimental lace and shoulder belt plate.

INDEX

Figures in **bold** refer to illustrations.